SUPER SPORTS
ALL-TERRAIN BIKES

DAVID JEFFERIS

Chrysalis Children's Books

First published in Great Britain in 2001 by
🌙 Chrysalis Children's Books
An imprint of Chrysalis Books Group
The Chrysalis Building, Bramley Rd
London W10 6SP
Paperback edition first published in 2003
Copyright © David Jefferis 2001

A Belitha Book

Design and editorial production
Alpha Communications
Educational advisor Julie Stapleton
Picture research Kay Rowley

ISBN 1 84138 345 7 (hb)
ISBN 1 84138 763 0 (pb)

British Library Cataloguing in Publication Data for this book is available from the British Library.

Printed in China
10 9 8 7 6 5 4 3 2 1 (hb)
10 9 8 7 6 5 4 3 2 1 (pb)

Acknowledgements
We wish to thank the following individuals and organizations for their help and assistance and for supplying material in their collections:
Action-Plus Photographic, Actionsnaps, Alpha Archive, Steve Bardens, Stewart Clarke, John Cleare, Matt Dickinson, DPPI, Darren England, Malcolm Fearon, Mike Hewitt, Mountain Camera Picture Library, Network Photographers, Gary Pearl, Mike Powell, Adam Pretty, Ben Radford, Jamie Squire, Michael Steele, Dave Stewart, Stock Shot, Joel Tribhout, F. Wagner, Nick Yates,

Diagrams by Gavin Page

▲ An all-terrain bike rider makes his bike do a 'wheelie' by lifting it off its front wheel.

Contents

Look out for the Super Sports symbol

Look for the cyclist silhouette in boxes like this.
Here you will find extra all-terrain bike facts,
stories and useful tips for beginners.

World of all-terrain bikes

▲ Some events test a rider's control of the bike at slow speeds.

All-terrain bikes are also called mountain bikes. They are sturdily built for riding on dirt trails and in the countryside.

All-terrain bikes, or ATBs, were first made in the 1970s for racing along dirt trails in the hills near San Francisco, USA.

Since then ATBs have taken over the cycling world. Today eight out of ten new bikes made are ATBs. They are used by commuters, weekend riders, explorers and for racing.

▲ Many riders don't want to race. They just enjoy a ride in the fresh air.

◀ Downhill races are held all year round. This rider is going down a snowy mountain slope.

▲ Cross-country races are across all sorts of difficult terrain, including streams and rivers.

◄ Mid-air jumps make ATB racing a great sport to watch. Here riders in a downhill event leap past red marker poles.

Looking at ATBs

There are hundreds of different types of all-terrain bikes, but they are all designed to be used on rough, uneven surfaces.

▲ Many ATBs have front shock absorbers (arrowed). These have springs inside that soak up the shock of hitting a bump.

The main part of an ATB is the frame. It is very strong and usually made of a metal, such as steel or aluminium. The frame supports other parts of the bike, such as the handlebars, wheels and pedals.

When bikes were made mostly for riding on roads, tyres and spokes were enough to cope with most bumps. ATBs are built for use on rougher ground, and many now have shock absorbers for the front or for both wheels. These make riding much smoother.

▲ 1950s cruiser bike.
▼ 2000s ATB bike.

Bicycles old and new

Today's ATB is very different from a bike made in the 1950s.

The cruiser bike (top left) was built for cycling in the streets. It has fat tyres, but the ATB's tyres (below left) also have chunky treads, for grip on dirt trails.

The cruiser bike has brakes that would not hold an ATB for a moment on a steep dirt slope. Today's machine has disc brakes, for much better stopping power, especially when a trail is muddy.

▲ Handlebar levers control the brakes. It's best to keep two fingers over each lever so you can brake quickly.

chain from pedals to rear wheel

▲ ATBs have chunky tyres, specially made for riding off the roads. The tyres dig into the soft ground to give a good grip.

▶ Most ATBs have 18 or 21 gears. Low gears are for starting off and for cycling up hills. High gears are for moving fast on flat ground.

Ready to ride

Before a trip, an all-terrain bike needs to be checked over. This includes pumping air into the tyres and oiling various parts.

▲ This ATB is ready to go! The tyres are pumped up and the moving parts oiled and greased.

If one of the bike's moving parts fails, you may have to cut your ride short and go home. So a well-prepared ATB rider has a set of tools and checks over the bike before setting off on a long run.
Punctures can happen, so it's important to take a repair kit along, including an air pump.

▼ A puncture repair kit should always be taken. Some riders use a spray can of foam to fill a hole in an emergency.

aerosol can fills
tyre with foam

puncture
repair kit

mini-pump fills a tyre
with air quickly

▲ On a warm summer day, a wet rider can dry off quickly. In winter, it's best to ride slowly through water to avoid getting soaked!

 Carrying an ATB

Cycling off the roads means that there are times when a rider has to get off the bike and carry it – perhaps to cross a stream or to climb a section that's too steep to ride.

The best way to carry an ATB is to bend your legs and put your arm under the top tube. Then straighten up with the bike resting on one shoulder.

top tube

On the trail

All-terrain biking may take riders a long way from home. So it's necessary to pack food and water, and a map to avoid getting lost.

▲ Car roof racks are useful for taking ATBs to and from off-road trails.

Riding a new trail is exciting, but it's best to do some research first. An up-to-date map is important, and it's worth checking that the planned route is open. Some trails may be shut to ATBs, especially in popular tourist spots.

Even on a short ride, riders should take food and drink. A small medical kit is also useful so cuts and scrapes can be treated quickly.

▼ Take a map, drink and food. Add a basic first-aid kit, just in case. A small camera is useful if the route is in a scenic area.

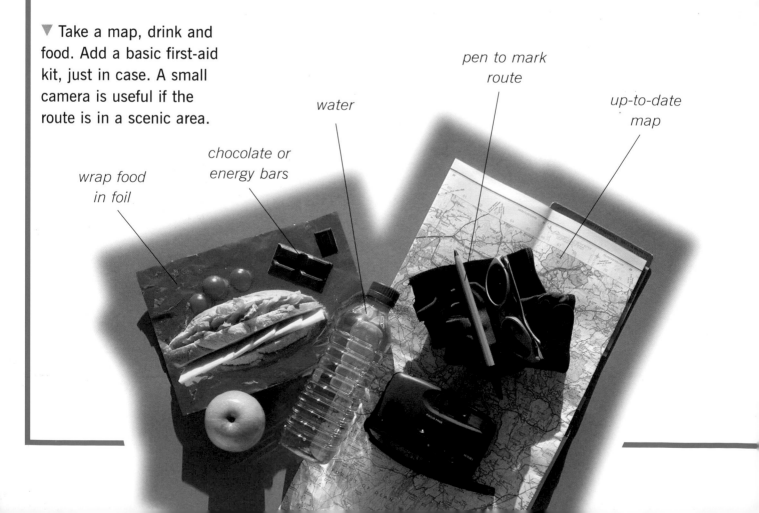

wrap food in foil

chocolate or energy bars

water

pen to mark route

up-to-date map

◀ A narrow trail in the Rocky Mountains of North America is an exciting ride. This is just a day trip, so the riders have no camping gear with them.

even a simple camera can give good results if the view is good

Photograph time

ATBs are great for getting away from cities and into the countryside.

A camera is handy for recording surprise moments, such as the sunset shown here.

Riders should make sure that front and rear lights are working. A return trip may be on roads in fading light, so lights will be needed for safety.

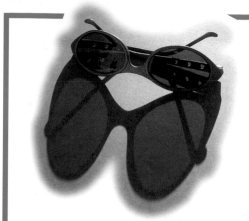

Safe riding

Staying safe is important when you're cycling. Keep your eyes on the trail, take care on steep slopes and wear a helmet.

▲ Sunglasses keep dust and insects out of the eyes. They also reduce eye strain.

The simplest way to avoid a fall is to check the trail ahead for dangers. Look out for loose or slippery surfaces on bends, and finish braking before making a turn so that the tyres don't lose their grip on the surface.

The best way to tackle a steep downhill section is to shift your body back and use the front brake to control your speed. If it still seems too steep, get off and walk!

◄ Steep sections can be ridden quickly but safely. The back brake does not work well down hills. The front brake helps the rider control the speed.

rider shifts back, to put his weight behind the saddle

GARY FISHER

▲ If you are carrying an ATB near water, keep it on the side nearest the land.

 **Fighting the cold**

Riding an all-terrain bike in winter is fun, but it can get chilly. A good way to warm cold fingers is by shaking them as if you are trying to shake off water. Stamping cold feet usually warms them up, but don't wear extra socks. Cramped shoes cut off blood circulation, so your feet get colder, not warmer.

Adventure ride

Day trips and weekend rides are not enough for some bikers. They like to go exploring far from home on their all-terrain bikes.

▲ Riders need to take great care near steep slopes or cliff tops.

It can be very exciting to go on a long trip to a distant place. The record is held by ATB riders who went from Britain to Australia, a distance of nearly 27 000 km. The journey, across Europe and Asia, raised over £15 000 for charity. The riders encountered blizzards and earthquakes. There was even a shipwreck when the ATBs were carried aboard a sailing ship!

► An ATB rider cycles across a stony plain, towards the Andes mountains in Peru, South America.

*pannier bags
carry baggage*

▲ Riders protect their heads from the sun in Africa's Sahara desert.

Covering the kilometres

Planning for any trip means allowing enough time to cover the distance. That includes thinking about the wind and weather, as well as the terrain.

A fit cyclist can cover about 120 km a day on smooth roads. On dirt tracks, 80-100 km is good going. On a muddy trail, it can be less than half this.

Downhill races

Off-road racing is a popular sport. High-speed downhill races are among the most exciting to watch.

Downhill races are over in a few minutes. Racers push their pedals down hard to speed along at 60 km/h or even faster.

Courses range from tracks through dark and muddy forests to trails down summer ski-slopes.

Organizers of downhill events often build sharp bends and steep ramps on the trail to add excitement to the race.

◄ This racing ATB has a disc brake for extra stopping power.

▲ Downhill racers crash often, so full-face helmets are worn for good head protection.

◄ Tyres slip and slide on loose gravel and stony surfaces, so riders take care on high-speed bends.

Slipping and sliding

The weather makes a big difference to downhill racing times. One rider in a competition in Switzerland said, 'Fog and thunderstorms wrecked my racing times. I took four minutes to go down the hill when we practised in dry weather. By the time we raced, heavy rain had turned the track into slimy mud – now I took over six minutes to race down!'

▲ Close-fitting glasses keep dust out of this rider's eyes.

Cross-country

Cross-country races take riders across routes that are so difficult that sometimes the bikes have to be carried.

Cross-country racing only started in the 1970s, but it is now included in the Olympic Games. Luckily you don't need to be an Olympic athlete to enjoy it!

There are races for all levels, including beginners. Cross-country racing classes are open for anyone who wants to ride, from primary school students to grandparents.

◄ Riders usually wear helmets with slots or vents. These let air flow on to the rider's head, to give a cooling effect.

bottle of water for drinking during the race

First-time racer

A cross-country race is a tough challenge for a beginner.

One first-time racer who entered a fun (easy) race had quite a shock. He thought the race would be little more effort than a weekend trail ride. 'But people cycled as if they were in the Olympics!', he said. 'I managed to come in fourth place. Boy, was I pleased!'

◄ Cross-country races include really rough parts where riders jump off and carry their ATBs.

Tough tests

Competition riding tests cyclists to their limits. Good training helps a rider to keep going and maybe even win the race.

▲ Some events have very hard sections in which riders have to haul their bikes all the way up steep hillsides.

Competition riders train to build up their fitness, strength and speed.

Fitness is needed if the rider is to keep going throughout a race. Strength is used to zoom up hills, especially the steep ones. And speed is needed to overtake other riders.

▲ Carrying an ATB towards the end of a race tests a rider's strength!

▶ Top riders try to pass slower ones as early as possible in a race. This leaves the course ahead clearer so they can move towards the front.

fingerless gloves protect backs and palms of hands

ATB fitness tips

Training steadily to build up body strength is the best way to get fit for an ATB race. For beginners, such training may be just riding regularly and racing against friends.

Losing body fluid through sweating is bad news, as this reduces muscle power. Some ATB racers suck drinking water from a slim tank, carried on the back like a rucksack.

BMX freestyle

BMX stands for bicycle moto-cross. In the 1970s these small-wheeled machines were the first bikes used for off-road races.

The first BMX bikes were fun machines, and were sold by the million. Today BMX bikes are ridden mostly in serious freestyle competitions. Freestyle is the skill of doing stunts, such as jumps and 'verting'. Here a rider takes off a steep ramp to do BMX tricks in mid-air.

▲ A rider does a freestyle stunt in mid-air. A good landing is just as important as the stunt.

▶ BMX riders mostly wear soft shoes so they can feel what the bike is doing. Full-face helmets are usually worn.

rider has pads to protect elbows and knees

BMX bike has smaller wheels than an ATB

▲ BMX riding is popular worldwide. Here a freestyler competes in the 'King of the Dirt' competition in Sydney, Australia.

 **BMX words**

Here are some popular words from the world of BMX riding:

Acrial   Any mid-air freestyle trick.
Endo   Balancing on the front wheel.
Peg   Metal extension from a wheel axle, used as a foot stand.
Pogo   Hopping a bike while balancing it on the front or rear wheel.
Vert   Vertical, the best angle off a launch ramp for freestyle tricks.

◄ Advanced riders can carry out aerial stunts like this.

New ideas

New all-terrain bikes and equipment are being developed all the time. New materials allow ATBs to be made lighter and stronger.

▲ Tiny flashing light units were first made in the 1990s. The extra-bright light makes a bike more visible at night.

Most future ATBs will have both front and rear shock absorbers to make riding easier on rough surfaces.

Frames made of aluminium or carbon fibre will be common. These materials are lighter and stronger than steel. Future ATBs will be better made and easier to ride, but will probably cost little more than those of today.

▼ These high-tech tools make repairs an easier job. Spanners and screwdrivers fold up small enough to tuck in a pocket. The 85 mm-long metal bottle holds enough air to inflate a tyre after repair.

fold-out screwdriver

fold-out spanner set

lyre pump and air bottle

▶ This design is for a police ATB. The equipment includes a medical kit, a radio and blue warning lights.

rear shock
absorber

front shock
absorber

◀ This machine has shock absorbers at front and back, for a smooth ride over rough ground. The frame is a lightweight design, with special high-power brakes.

lightweight
pedals

ATB facts

▲ The célerifère was the world's first bicycle.

Here are some facts and stories from the world of all-terrain bikes.

Early riders

Bicycles go back to the late eighteenth century. In 1791, the French Count de Sivrac built a two-wheeled wooden horse, which he called a célerifère. It was popular for a while, but had no steering, no brakes, and no pedals. In the 1860s a bicycle with pedals was built, by the Michaux brothers, in Paris, France. Michaux bikes had no gears, so they were quite slow.

Squashy tyres

Early bikes had solid wheels, which made them very uncomfortable to ride – many early bicycles were called 'boneshakers', because of this. In 1881 Scotsman John Dunlop invented the first pneumatic tyre. It was made of rubber, and filled with air to give a softer ride over bumps. Pneumatic tyres made riding so much better that they have been used ever since.

First ATBs

All-terrain bicycles were first developed in the 1970s, when keen riders went racing down hilly trails in California, USA. These bikes were hand-built, and were called 'klunkers', because they seemed heavy and clumsy compared to the lightweight road bikes of the time.

◄ An ATB tyre is made with a deep pattern called a tread. This gives lots of grip on soft ground.

thick rubber tread

◄ Climbing hills is hot work, especially in summer.

Bunny hops

A bunny hop is when a rider jerks a bike's front and back wheels in turn off the ground, to jump over an obstacle. Bunnies were first perfected by BMX riders, and now ATB riders do them too. The world record is for a hop 112.5 cm off the ground.

Oldest ATB race

Despite its name, the Road Apple Rally is an off-road ATB race. It was started in 1981, and has been held every year since. The idea behind the first Rally was to cycle as far as a horse could cover in one day – about 20 km across rough country – in one hour.

Saving weight

ATB riders have tackled many long-distance trips around the world. On one two-month journey two riders were so keen to save weight that they took no tent or cooking gear. They also removed designer labels from their clothes and cut off the unprinted edges of their trail maps.

Drink up

ATB riding is an energetic sport, which involves sweating away body fluid. The body is made mostly of water, so it's essential not to lose too much, otherwise a rider can feel faint or be sick. When riding hard, a rider needs to drink about a litre of water an hour.

Friendly to the environment

The bicycle is probably the most efficient vehicle ever invented. A cyclist can ride over 500 km, using about the same energy as there is in a litre of petrol. A typical small car can travel about 20 km on the same amount.

► This is an ATB with a difference. Instead of wheels, the Austrian machine has skis, and is built for riding on snow, sand or even grass.

▲ A BMX freestyle trick.

ATB words

Here are some technical terms used in this book.

aluminium

A silvery-white metal that is strong, yet light in weight.

ATB

Letters that stand for all-terrain bike. ATBs are often called mountain bikes.

BMX

Letters that stand for bicycle moto-cross. BMX bikes are smaller and lighter than ATBs. They were first used in the cycling version of moto-cross, an off-road motorcycle sport.

carbon fibre

A material used in various parts of an ATB. Carbon fibre is usually a plastic with small hairs of carbon added. It is strong and light.

cross-country

An ATB race that takes place on a winding course, usually with some sections too difficult to ride. Here riders get off and carry their machines.

disc brake

Brake with two pads that grip either side of a metal disc. Cars and motorcycles have used them for many years, but they have been made for ATBs only since the 1990s.

downhill

A type of ATB race which takes place on a winding trail going down a hill. Dual races include both downhill and cross-country sections.

frame

Metal 'backbone' of an ATB, made of strong tubes that are joined together, usually in a triangular design. On cheap bikes the frame is often made of steel. More expensive bikes may have frames of aluminium or carbon fibre, which are lighter in weight.

freestyle

The sport of making a BMX bike do mid-air tricks.

◀ Most cycle frames have a triangle design because it is very strong.

full-face helmet

A type of helmet that covers the head completely for the best all-round protection in a crash. The wearer looks out through an eye-slit in the front of the helmet.

gear

System of cogs used on a bike to make pedalling easier. Low gears are used for starting off and for cycling up hills. High gears are for speeding along on the flat and for cycling down hills.

handlebar

Metal cross-tube used to steer a bike. Gear and brake controls are next to the handgrips at each end.

Olympic Games

International games that are held every four years.

pneumatic tyre

Tyre that that has an inner rubber tube, filled with air. The inner tube gives slightly to absorb the shock of riding over bumps.

▲ Pneumatic tyres and front shock absorbers give this ATB a smooth ride.

shock absorber

A cylinder holding a metal spring, designed to soak up bumps. Many ATBs now have two shock absorbers, one either side of the front wheel. More expensive ATBs have one for the back wheel, too.

terrain

Another word for ground.

tread

Pattern of rubber, moulded in a tyre. On an ATB, the tread lets the tyre sink slightly into the ground for good grip, especially in mud.

wheelie

Pulling the front wheel off the ground for a few moments, while keeping the bike balanced on the back wheel.

▲ Many downhill ATBs use disc brakes (arrowed).

ATB science

These experiments show you some of the science in the world of all-terrain bikes.

▲ This bike has a pair of front shock absorbers.

Bouncing over the bumps

A bike with shock absorbers gives a controlled ride. Inside the metal tube of each shock absorber is a spring that soaks up bumps on the trail.

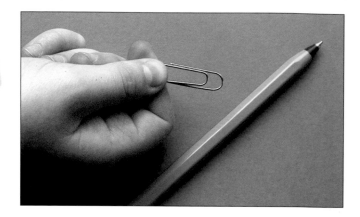

1 For this mini-experiment all you need is a metal paper clip and a thin tube. A ballpoint pen is just right for the job.

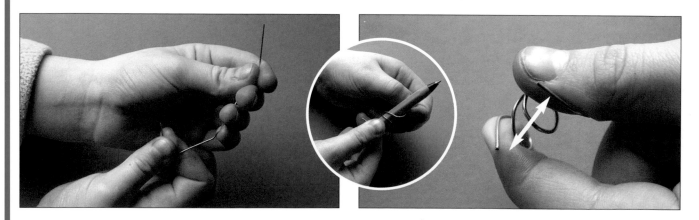

2 Carefully straighten out the paperclip. Hold one end against the ballpoint pen with your thumb. Wrap the clip around the pen.

3 You should end up with a metal spiral. Slide it off the pen, and gently squeeze it between your fingers. Feel the springy bounce!

▲ Oiling moving parts keeps a bike in good condition for riding.

Oil keeps things apart

The moving parts of a bike, such as the wheels, gears and chain, need to be oiled often.

The oil flows in a thin film between metal parts to reduce friction, the rubbing action when things touch each other.

1 You need a kitchen cutting board and a square block for this experiment. Here the block is made from toy building bricks.

2 Lay the block on the board and flick it with your finger. The block moves, but soon stops. Now pour a little oil on the board.

3 You will find that a flick now sends the block much further. The oil reduces friction by keeping the block and board slightly apart.

Index